LUBOV

The Heart Of The Beloved

Catherine
de Hueck Doherty

LIVING FLAME PRESS
BOX 74 LOCUST VALLEY, N.Y. 11560

Cover: Robert Manning

Illustrations: Donna Surprenant

Published by: Living Flame Press
              Box 74
              Locust Valley, N.Y. 11560

ISBN: 0-914544-60-8

Printed in the United States of America

Dedication

To my son, George

Introduction

"For what human being can understand a man's thoughts except that person himself?" (1 Corinthians 2:11).

Throughout the years to come, people will be criticizing, organizing and attempting to give interpretations to the life, work and spiritual doctrine of Catherine Doherty. Having been deeply immersed in the editing and study of Catherine's writings over the past decade, it is my conviction that what we have in these pages are the most profound and intimate expressions of the heart of this great woman of our times.

I have always been amazed at the variety of forms her writings can assume. She has expressed her gospel vision in powerful prophetic utterances, in straightforward and strong teachings, in stories from her life, in imaginative parables, or, as in I Live on an Island (Ave Maria Press, 1979), she simply gazes upon nature and speaks to us of the truths of God reflected there. She can write general letters of guidance to her spiritual children, or, she can write personal, intimate letters to any individual in need of her wisdom.

What and who is she, then? A lecturer? A prophet? A teacher? A counselor? A spiritual mother? Yes, she is all of these; but in essence what and who is she? She tells us herself:

> You ask me, who am I? I am the echo of a voice. You ask me, who am I? I am a breath, a wind. You ask me, who am I? I am a flame. You ask me, who am I? I am a tear. You ask me, who am I? I am a sinner God has touched. You ask me, who am I? I'll answer you: A fool in love with God.

I am a song caught by the wind . . . a dancer
on the sea of eternity . . . I am a woman in love
with God.

This is essentially who she is . . . a woman pas-
sionately in love with God. Her life and work are a
lavish and extravagant throwing of her whole being at
the feet of Christ, singing and singing (as she likes to
quote St. Francis) that she has given God such a small
thing. All her literary forms are ways she seeks, with
the ingenuity of love, to make her Beloved more known
and loved.

The deepest utterances of a lover take place in the
private and intimate conversations with the Beloved.
That is what we have in the poems, meditations, heart
talks of Catherine Doherty. We have the cor ad cor lo-
quitur, the heart speaking to Heart, the poor woman
who was chosen to be the bride of the great King, pour-
ing out her love to Him. I believe that any interpreta-
tion of Catherine's teachings in the future must be
firmly rooted in these interior conversations.

Catherine never intended these for publication.
They were written in that silent intimacy of lovers for
the sole purpose of communion with her Beloved. She
is not conscious of a world audience, or of the need to
direct her thoughts for the guidance of others. No. She
is simply resting on her Beloved's heart, communing
with herself and with Him. She is absorbed in His
presence and in His love. From this place close to God's
heart comes her deepest outpouring of love, pain,
outrage at the Beloved's neglect by others; and the
Beloved feeds her with His deepest wisdom about life,
about the state of the world and about His own
loneliness and pain.

The reading of and meditation upon these interior
conversations have, of all Catherine's writings, drawn

me personally most profoundly into her own mind and heart. What is more, they have drawn me into her own profound relationship with God. I assure you, you are in for one of the most awesome revelations of a person's interior life you have ever been privileged to share.

It takes courage to expose one's interior life to the indiscriminate gaze of thousands. May everyone read these conversations with the same delicacy and gentleness, with the same reverence and love, with which they were spoken to the Beloved.

Finally, I wish to share with you a poem Catherine wrote for me on the occasion of my final promises here at Madonna House in December 1979:

You wait before unknown gates, not knowing why nor whence this request has come to you — to wait upon unknown gates!

It moves — as time will always move toward its goal which is eternity — or shall we say Eternal. And still you wait before those unknown gates, in faith and patience, which grows day by day.

It seems to you at times the gates are opening — just a little. It may be you will know what is behind them. But still you wait because of faith, because of love and hope, you wait before unknown gates!

Then, quite suddenly, the gates become immense; and yet, while they are so immense, they seem to be small too — a paradox again. And still you wait.

But now the gates are open.
Your hands are touching two handles of the gates, because it seems to you they must be

6

quite open. And suddenly, you look upon your hands, and lo, behold, you see that they are not immense gates, nor small ones either.

They simply are the handles of God's heart that you can open now to enter in.

Robert Wild
Priest of Madonna House
February 14, 1984
Harlem Foundation Day
Combermere, Ontario

Table of Contents

1

The Pain of Christ

The Pain of Christ

Have you, beloved friends, felt the pain of Christ which is all around you? It is because it covers me, encompasses me, that I write to you. For I cannot rest, nor can I be silent before this immense, overwhelming pain of Christ in our brethren.

I have looked on it for the many years of my life. I have realized too that each year my eyes have seen deeper into that pain, recognized it quicker, wept over it longer and desired with an ever-growing desire to assuage it faster.

I have seen it in the hurt eyes of black children playing in the garbage-infested alleyways in the Harlems of America. I have seen it in the hopeless posture of a Mexican mother, thin and gaunt, who held a sickly babe to her milkless breast.

I have seen it in the empty, impassive face of an Indian trudging patiently over the empty desert. I have caught its song in the high-pitched voices of restless children whose playground was a deadly city street. I have heard its pleading voice in the voices of men and women whose loneliness touched mine.

I have drowned in it when listening to youth in our beautiful land, mouthing words of hatred and denial of God, calling other men to join them in their crusade of hatred and destruction. Foolish, deluded youth who began the search for love and truth and somewhere along the line were given stones for bread.

I have slept with the pain of Christ among the poor, poor myself, sharing with three other girls, tired and hungry, a bed too narrow for two. I have walked with the pain of Christ along a beautiful, shady country road, listening to a dirge from the lips of a farmwife whose family was hopelessly lost in a network of sickness, mortgages and soulless red tape.

Yes, I have touched, seen, heard and slept with the pain of Christ for almost as many years as I have lived. There was a time when I had something to give to assuage this intolerable pain of my God and yours. I had a life to give to it, for it. But now, today, I myself am poor. Behold my poverty. My life, I have given and with it myself, my waking and sleeping hours.

But, Lord of love, it is so little to give and I stand before you as I am, bereft of any gifts to give while the sea of your pain rises, rises round about me, ever higher. I look to see if there is anything left to give and I stand before you as I am.

And so, beloved friends, here I am, lifting my voice for you to hear, asking, imploring, beseeching for the wherewithal to assuage the pain of Christ in our brethren.

I Saw the Lord

I saw the Lord hungry and cold and shelterless. I could not rest. I had to take him into my arms to give him comfort. But lo, when I did, it was not God but just a child, hungry and cold.

I saw the Lord bleeding and sick. I could not rest. So I arose to assuage his pain. But lo, when I did, it was not God but just a wasted man in pain.

I saw the Lord weeping alone in a new Gethsemani I had not seen before. I could not rest. I had to go and share his tears and woes. But lo, when I did, it was not God but just a beggar-woman by the road.

I Love You, Christ

I love you, Christ of mystery and flame. I love you utterly. Utterly surrendered, I rest at peace in mystery and fire, knowing only that this is my place. I love you, Christ, desired one of nations, whose prefiguration began with the dawn of time.

I love you, Christ of mystery and flame. My loving eyes seem to pierce time, beholding your beauty slowly revealing itself against the folds of time.

I love you, Christ of mystery and flame. Bridegroom of souls, in your arms I rest, a soul in love. Oh great love, how can such a small thing as I find a nestling place within your embrace?

I love you, Christ of mystery and flame. Of the forgotten, the lost, the lonely and the sick. In them, I see your beauty with a strange ecstasy full of pain.

I love you, Christ of mystery and flame. Lord of splendors I cannot encompass or comprehend. Yet childlike I venture to your side unmindful of the hosannaing crowds.

I love you, Christ of mystery and flame. Love you with a passion that spills in torrents from my soul and changes into a white flame of pain when I behold you crucified, bleeding for the sins of all.

I love you, Christ of mystery and flame. Christ of Calvary which is our mystery of love. I know, for the pain of it fills me to overflowing. It seems as if I know the smell and feel of nails encrusted with your blood that dried in the noonday sun.

I love you, Christ of mystery and flame. Christ of Calvary, it seems I know the feel of wood, each ridge uneven, each groove. It seems to me I hang on it, myself alone, dying for love of you.

16

I love you, Christ of mystery and flame. God of poverty sublime that is so rich. I love you, carpenter of Nazareth, smelling of sweat.

I love you, Christ of mystery and flame, my Lord and God, with all of me. I have forgotten all the past. The future? What is that? I love but for this minute, this instant, when, reposing on your heart, I hear your heartbeats telling me you love me too, while I can go and do "the duty of the instant, of the moment," for you.

I Knew You Then

I know you, Lord, though I have never seen your face. I knew you, Lord. You came to me, a man without grace. Your face was blotched and swollen. You wore cast-offs that in the long ago adorned some man of substance; your pants were held up by strings, or were they cords? I knew you then.

I know you, Lord, though I have never seen your face. I knew you, Lord, in the fat, sloppy woman next door throwing another pail of garbage into her yard. Her face was fat and white. (The poor eat too many carbohydrates; they are so cheap.) I knew you then.

Yes, I know you, Lord, even though I have never seen your face. I knew you in the children playing in the dirty, rat-infested alleyways of city slums. There were no other places for them to play. I knew you then.

I knew you in the faces of prostitutes, sellers of "love," hungry for Love. I knew you in the million faces of youth in search of you, in priests who never met you, in nuns who looked as if they did but never had. I knew you then.

Yes, I knew you in a thousand faces, though never having seen your human face. I saw you in a thousand faces and loved you beyond all words — Rabboni!

But now you come to me in storms. You are like thunder, lightning, wind that tears at me as if you were a lover in a hurry to tear me out by the roots and transplant me somewhere upon some mountain, alone with you.

You come to me like a sharp sword, to cut me off from all you bade me do and be, even from all those you brought to me, to bring to you.

You come at noonday and it becomes a night so dark

that earth's bowels look bright against your night. You lift me up. You throw me down, as if I was a ball you played with.

Lord of nights, lightning, storms and thunder, what is this tearing of me asunder? What roads have you in mind for me to travel? What mountains must I climb? And why the silence?

Ecce Homo

I let you in today. You were disguised; but then, perhaps you weren't at all. They fettered you with chains of selfishness. They wrapped you up with a cloak of their shallowness. They crowned you again with the crown of their thoughtlessness. And then, they brought you in.

And I beheld you thus. Then you vanished from my sight and all I could see was cloak and chain and crown, not as they were, but as they showed me each.

Quite suddenly I understood you were in pain. The only thing that I could do was then to love the selfish, the thoughtless and the cold.

My feet had wings and I began to serve. For love serves without counting the cost, the selfish and the thoughtless and the cold, because they bear within their souls yourself, my Lord, yourself, all chained and crucified and crowned with thorns again.

Christ's Lament

I walk the streets of crowded cities. So few I meet who know my name. I walk the scented fields of the country, yet no one greets me with a kind word.

I am a stranger to those for whom I died a thousand deaths one sunny afternoon.

I long to rest upon the hearts of those who are my own. But I find them too busy to stop and give me rest. They say they are busy about my business or that of my Father, but what a lie! They waste the time of which I am the Master. They squander it so lavishly, forgetting that I shall ask account of every thought and deed, of every second, minute, hour.

Who then will open their heart to me? For I am weary and want to rest. Isn't there somewhere just one apostle who will share loneliness and weariness once more with me?

2

Pilgrim

I Am a Wanderer

He asked me once, long ago, if I would love him as he loved me. Young, gay, joyous, I answered, "Yes, indeed!" Then he smiled and for a wedding ring, he gave me his pain.

Since then, I have not slept. My soul refuses all rest. It is aflame with one desire — to heal his pain.

I have become an outcast of love and fire. My desire urges me on. My heart is a fiery dart that flies into his heart and falls back on earth to shed his fire.

I wonder as I wander . . . where shall I find oils and balms to heal his pain? True, I am a beggar but I know that gold and silver will not buy love's healing.

I know that I must pierce my heart and die of love. Drop by drop my blood will mingle with his. The mingling will be the only balm he will take to heal his wounds.

Pink Room

I wept again in anguish. I wept in a pink room set for a bride, with curtains fine and pictures fair and ladies of expensive porcelain standing here and there.

I wept because a naked Christ was dying everywhere in bare or cluttered rooms. It seemed to me the world shrank into a barren cell adorned with a crucifix and God dying on it.

And here I was in my pink room, dying with him amidst curtains fine and pictures fair and ladies of expensive porcelain standing here and there.

A Pilgrim of Silence and Pain

I am a pilgrim of your pain.

You walked barefoot on the dusty roads of Palestine, the Palestine that was so small. I, your pilgrim, travel on ships and planes, on roads and streets, across the sea, the air, the land, to which your Palestine would be a little nook, a square, a tiny part of an immense kaleidoscopic whole.

And yet your footprints are everywhere, and I, I walk in them. My steps are slow, for I am wounded too, even as you, by you, my love, for you and them. The wounds drip, drop by drop, on ship, on land and in the air. My blood — or is it your blood in me? — falls everywhere.

Gone are the days of speech, of just and flaming anger, of words like swords in your defense. Today I speak in silence and through my wounds — or are they yours? Alone among the noisy crowds I am a pilgrim of silence and of pain. And everywhere I leave a gift, a drop or two of blood, not knowing any more if it be mine or yours.

I am a pilgrim seeking you, yet giving you to all. For it is you, my Lord, who meets me in each one I see or touch or pass. How strange and how incredible. A mystery so profound and I so small and foolish.

I lose you in so many, Lord, for they will not welcome you into their houses. And I run again, with wounds that bleed, with wounds that gape a little more with every step. I run on and on, for I must find you, and at the same time I must give you to all I see and meet and touch.

Yes, I must find you and give you to all, through silence and through pain. Alleluia!

27

I Am a Pilgrim
of the Absolute

I am a pilgrim, a pilgrim of the Absolute, a strange, unnoticed pilgrim who walks, yet always somehow stands still. I am an innkeeper whose joy and gladness is to pick the stranger up, the stranger who was beset by robbers, and take him into the inn that is my heart.

Yes, I am an innkeeper and a pilgrim, always in motion yet standing still. No gold or silver do I carry but only gourds of wine, the wine of love, and vessels filled with oils, the oils of compassion.

Yes, I am a pilgrim of the Absolute, who always walks and yet stands still.

A Lay Apostle

Young, eager, strong and unafraid, touched by the fire of the Crimson Dove, dreaming a thousand dreams in God, of love, of souls . . . mystic untried yet true, in love with love.

Recklessly loving without counting costs, sells all he owns and poorer than the modern poor of welfare states, embraces cross and thorny crown, as men do women when love and passion meet. A man aflame, shedding with every step fire on earth, the fire of his heart and Pentecost, burning youth, strength, only to be renewed in both as an eagle.

Time slowly moves, each year leaving its burning seal upon his wounded heart. Now days are grayer, mists swirl in a strange motion that is more sensed than seen. With them come doubts and pain and poverty bites deep, as does a strange fatigue that smothers joy and leaves a lassitude that kills all fire, passion, desire.

Then comes the night, dark, unserene, disturbed and stormy. Now all hell is loose. There is no light. Fear stalks the footsteps of him who knew no fear. Alone he walks amongst the cold, hate-filled hearts of men and hears the whistling sound that stones make as they are hurled through the air by angry hands of men so filled with hate that their hearts are harder than the stones they hurl.

Now, poverty is master of him who thought of her as friend. Now he understands that he is nothing, and alone, a fool if ever man was but yet a fool for Christ. Alone, abandoned to the night, yet loving still, with pain racking him in body and in soul, yet loving still, he now begins to understand the price of souls.

Now years become as water, relentlessly washing him away. He feels as if he were not and yet he knows he is. If you were to ask, he would reply, "I am so empty that I live not . . . but Christ now lives in me."

He does not know as yet that this is the moment of his beginning. Now he can start. But no, not he . . . Christ will. Now time stands still. The bridge is made. The Kingdom of the Lord again has come to earth. The lay apostle now has come of age.

3

Virtues

Beauty

I have seen beauty in the deathless green of cedars and in autumn's crimson sheen but never quite so soulful or so fair as when I find her by an alley stair where children call and patient women hum a dreary day away when night has come.

I have seen magic in a young man's eyes who dwelt in a tenement yet shared the skies; have held my breath while once a noon sun flung its brush of saffron on a clothesline hung between dark windows; and I marveled when the stars spilled silver on its cloth again.

I have seen beauty in a plain, clean room where all love's flowers bloom for two old hearts and where more light has shone than churns on moonlit seas, white and alone. And once, down a dusty back road, I found the Christ where Magdalene wept on the ground.

You best will find her where the people plod, for beauty walks where walk the sons of God.

Chastity

The theologians spoke in learned words. Chastity, they said, was continency. It was aloof. It kept itself apart. It lived on pinnacles, snowy white, difficult of access, reached by few.

They pondered further amidst austere, cold rooms of ancient cities and comfy ones of new metropolises. They took chastity apart and when they were done, they put it back together again. It seemed so lusterless, so cold, dead somehow, perhaps from too much handling.

A prostitute was strolling down the street, mascaraed eyes were kind and painted mouth tender, soft; the swaying body, young. A small child came up to her and said, "You smell so nice. I like you." The girl blushed and bent to kiss the little face, so pure, so innocent. The kiss was chastity itself. It shone like blinding light.

A gay, singing, pony-tailed woman-child was walking by. She sang a jazzy song. A man stopped, turned and followed her, his heart full of lust. But then she turned. He looked into her eyes and quickly walked on, for chastity had smiled at him in the fullness of its purity.

A mother of a brood came next, heavy of body and step, burdened with a lot of bags and one infant, chubby, heavy. Men smiled and women too, for chastity was passing by, fruitful and full. The theologians did not know the face of chastity, for they had cut her up to see what made her tick.

Littleness

Beloved, you know well my foolish heart. You have beheld its foolishness so long, you will not mind beholding it again in all its littleness and fears, bewilderments and tiny pains.

Beloved, I am so truly small and worth nothing at all, except in you.

My smallness is all right. It fits your hand well and you know that you possess it so utterly as to absorb it fully. But you love to let me go into a cloud where knowledge does not dwell and where all things are still and wrapped in love and you.

I love the cloud, the silence, the love and you; and I love the pain, the darkness and the strange rain of things that happen by your will to me when you desire that I should retire from the cloud and go to search for your footprints in the dark of men's souls.

Listen to me! Utter foolishness talking to you who are all wisdom, all might, all light! But small things that fit your hand are unafraid of all these things and talk right up to you who are all love and tenderness and who deigns to stoop to littleness and scoop it into your arms.

So I keep on telling you what little foolish hearts think when you let them speak into your ear.

The cloud of "not knowing," the dark, the rain, the pain, the cold, the tempter's laugh, his loathsome touch, the slimy things of hell, the dank rivers of pride, so still, so black, the pains that come and go, the wood that holds me tight — oh Love, for you and souls, give those to me and I will call them joyous ecstasies.

Atonement

The host is passive. So am I. The host is love; a novice I. My novitiate, the hands of priests. Some are filled with love, some filled with greed, some full of self, some full of God, some swollen with lust or pride, some humble like a blade of grass, some empty like a rusty flask.

I lie within those priestly hands and rest with all that is best; or I undergo, in their hands, the torture of the damned.

It does not matter, for I know that only thus will I become one with host and God; for only thus will I be lifted up and grow in love, in unity with him who is so white, so small, so passive, so immense.

And I know more. As priestly hands touch me and bring me joy or agony, in some strange manner I can atone, becoming something strange that draws upon itself their pain, temptations, sins. For I too have become a piece of bread, absorbing good wine and bad, for love of him, for love of priests who are himself.

Behold then, friend, a mystery of unity, of pain, of joy, of many things that no human words can tell.

Simplicity

You speak so easily of her they call simplicity. But do you know the way to her?

It too is simple, like herself. Two beams that make a cross are simple, homey things to make of trees that grow abundantly. Three nails, so easily come by, so cheap, so simple. A hammer, an old familiar tool, will do nicely too. Now your hands and feet, simple familiar parts of you.

You will find simplicity. The way will be quite simple, straight and clear, when wood and nails and you are one. Then she is yours.

A Strange Fire

Love is a strange fire. It burns now vividly, flamboyantly; now banking fire and light, it is just a tender, bright glow in the dark.

Before a breath, a sigh, has come and gone, it changes into hunger that turns inward and consumes without consuming. A hunger that urges on to depths, to heights unscaled by men, it knows no obstacle. Its running outdistances sound and wind; and yet it can be still as dead things are still, or live as vibrantly as music does, or youth.

The face of love is hidden behind an endless caravan of faces. Its hunger and its fire change it into the face that needs it and will find peace in beholding it.

It dies a thousand deaths in one second and yet is resurrected before it knows the tomb. It is of time, yet its home is beyond all time. It spans eternity and is at home in it.

Love walks all roads and stands at all crossroads. The walking and the standing are part of loving, for everywhere men seek it at all times. And yet when they find it, they do not know its worth. They use it for their solace and then they leave it lightly, not even knowing the wounded, bleeding thing they left behind.

But love does not die. It is again on fire and ready to light their path. They do not know that its heat and warmth are an endless holocaust.

Obedience

Obedience is the crown of poverty and a footstool of charity. Obedience is the song of love expressed in deeds. Obedience is the supreme loyalty to the Beloved.

Obedience made God human but makes man divine. Obedience is cruciform for both God and man and therefore is the marriage bed of the Lover and the beloved. Obedience is joyful surrender to the Lover. Obedience is the freedom of the beloved, for the heart of the Lover belongs to it.

Obedience is the eternally renewed poem, not written in words but in little things done well for the love of the Beloved, throughout one's lifetime until death, when obedience folds her wings and departs, as does poverty and chastity, leaving Lover and beloved in a perfect union of love.

4

Silence, Solitude

Apostolate of Love

Be still, oh soul of mine. Listen to the great silence of the Lord. Be still and listen, becoming pregnant with his love.

Be still. Listen. In pain, travail and agony, give birth to other souls, fruits of his silence and his love.

And now, arise and go about his Father's business and lead your children into his paths. Then, oh happy soul, you have brought forth the Lord's apostolate of love.

My Cell

My cell is wide, as wide as streets and country lanes. Its walls are the open marketplaces of foggy cities or towering mountaintops of the far north; its roof, the ceilings of shops, log cabins or igloos.

My days are spent in service to foe and friend. I live in noise chaotic, strident, of traffic dense or in the endless silence of forests, fields and crooked country lanes.

I am bereft of outward silence and privacy refuses to dwell with me. For a thousand eyes, curious and cold, frightening and bold, strip and nail me upon a low cross.

Open is my resting place. Open is my eating place. Open is the whole of me — ready to be eaten up; ready to be called upon to feed the hungry, clothe the naked, nurse the dying, visit the prisons, comfort the lonely, the lame and the blind. Such is the life of a lay apostle.

But lo, walk softly through the secret doors of my heart. No matter where my feet take me, no matter what task is in my hands, my soul is steeped in solitude; it is alone with God. Silence enfolds my heart and soul. Silence makes of them convent and cell where the Lord dwells.

The Martha in me walks streets and lanes. The Mary in me rests and waits — a garden enclosed — for his delights, peaceful and fragrant, silent and lost in the waiting.

The Martha in me scrubs a hundred floors, nurses and cooks, and does endless chores.

Mary in me knows ecstasy in his embrace.

Martha in me sews and knits, writes and does all that she must to bring to all the face of him who rests on Mary's breast within.

Christ's Supper

We sup together in silence. We weep together in silence. He returns from whence he came and I seek more charcoal for the next fire.

Yes, I need much charcoal or kindling or something to start the fire once more. For the Lord comes again and again and again, in so many disguises and always he is hungry and thirsty. I must give him to eat. I must give him to drink.

Let me hurry to find the charcoal, the kindling. For I hear already his steps.

Fiat

My heart and I, Beloved, are lost in the immensity of inner silence, inner solitude. We do not try to find our way out of it. It seems we are too tired to move, so we stay quite still.

Yet it is not the warm silence of your voice, which we know can be heard without sounds or words. Nor is it the solitude we crave because it is in you, away from worldly noise.

No, it is the silence of many strange pains, doubts that press and sear and tear us apart, my heart and I. It is the solitude of the pariahs who walk alone, despised of men, seemingly forgotten by God.

Yet we do not try to find our way out of it, my heart and I. We stay where we are put because of a small word we said once, said once to you, meaning it with our whole heart — "Fiat!"

It is that little word that alone keeps us so still within the heavy silence, the deadly solitude.

Alone

Alone, in solitude, I speak when the night is deep, the fire low and I am sure no one will know.

Alone, in solitude, I speak. To whom, I do not know. And yet it seems a loving voice answers my thoughts and shares with me my tears, my dreams and ecstasies.

Alone, in solitude, I speak.

Neon Signs and Stars

A neon sign blotting out, with its red-purples, a shining star . . . the raucous cry of horns, the swish of endless cars silence the music of ocean waves reflecting stars.

Canned music from coffee houses, cocktail lounges, orange drink stands and eateries, sleezy or chic, drown the songs of breezes, cool and sweet.

Men are schizophrenied by all these. You see them, God, lost, divided against themselves. For neon signs, horns, canned music have muted your voice until man is a corpse who walks in California.

48

5

My Joys

Familiar Sounds

The earth is nigh and life flows by, full of familiar sounds: a door slamming somewhere, a voice calling out to shut the door, the snatches of some new and tender song, steps on a stairway, laughter, the clanking of a spoon against a cup, the sound of rain upon the roof.

Yet the earth is far, far away; the night is light, a path leading up, up, unto some mountain top as yet unseen. Now all sound ceases. Silence reigns, silence and light, leading my soul up, up a path to some mountain top as yet unseen.

And then, quite suddenly, a door that was not there opens wide and my soul enters the kingdom of light, of love, of joy. It is the kingdom of the mercy of the Lord, all tender, green and flowery, like gardens in the spring.

Such is the mercy of the Lord, all filled with tenderness. The grass is velvet under my feet. The trees are shady and bring merciful relief to a skin blackened by a desert's heat. The breeze is gentle with a scent unknown on earth.

But what is this? Again, familiar sounds: a door slamming somewhere, a voice calling, steps on a stairway, laughter, the clinking of a spoon against a cup.

My soul is back.

Northern Lights

The northern lights make wondrous cathedrals in the night. Their domes are heaven, air their walls, with colonnades of light, painted rainbows of delight.

The northern lights make wondrous cathedrals in the night where choirs are colors, where songs are movement of a blending of night, of light.

Why do the northern lights make cathedrals of the night? So as to remind the sons of men that all the universe worships the Lord of hosts.

Ecstasy

Some time ago that seems but yesterday, a giant soul cried out in ecstasy, "Out of the flesh or in the flesh, I know not."

Since then, men, through all the days and years in between his cry and our day, have tried to fathom God's unfathomable ways — and all in vain.

For the Lord reveals his secrets as he wills and those who hear his voice are dumb and deaf and blind to anything or anyone but him.

Men think they understand when giant souls cry out, and learnedly discuss and even write about the words, the tone, the notes. They even try to analyze the essence of their ecstasy.

Oh foolish "little learned men," you do not know you deal in straw. For giant souls are small and do not understand anything. The only thing they know is that the Lord touched their house of sod and for a second or two — or was it a day, or even an eternity — it fell away from them and they were free to see without seeing and hear without hearing and know in an immense, unknowing way, the touch of God.

Perhaps they cried out loud; perhaps they whispered in their dark and blinding night. It mattered not, for all they knew was that they were lost in God.

If ecstasy was theirs, they did not analyze, experiment, lament the lack of paper and of pen. They simply ceased to be, for ecstasy is love and love is God again.

Star Dust

My thoughts are scattered in the night, pinpoints of light, inverted heaven full of stars.

Oh passer-by, bend down and take a handful of my star dust. It may become a light to make your dark days bright.

My thoughts are scattered in the night, pinpoints of light, inverted starlit heaven.

Oh you who hunger and thirst, take my star dust. It will lead you to one who assuages all hunger and all thirst.

White Flame

White flame, resplendent in infinite humility, merges with simplicity supreme . . . small, yet beyond all measuring! Imprisoned in a monstrance, the host stands still. Yet, from it shines power intense and it draws all to infinite and perfect rest.

White flame, resplendent, blinding the sight of souls that love! Whiteness, stillness from whence love incarnate sends the fire of a thousand million desires that stem from it.

White flame, resplendent, sings of its hunger for souls in words of fire unheard by multitudes but calling, calling to those whose hearts expand beneath the touch of its white sun.

White flame, resplendent, changes to a thousand colors of pity, love, desire, mercy's cleansing fire. Behold the host imploring souls for love. Behold the Pauper from above with palms extended, begging for the worn-out coins of human hearts. Pause and see the supreme Beggar begging from thee a word, a glance of love, a chance to rest within your human breast.

White flame, resplendent, bends low to impart the secret of its flame and as it does, the flame ignites my heart and I become, myself, the secret of hidden love.

There is no space, there is no time. I and my Lover divine are one flame. I am pierced by the sword of his love, absorbed by the fierce desire of his fire that penetrates me unto eternity.

Who Am I?

You ask me, who am I? I am the echo of a voice. You ask me, who am I? I am a breath, a wind. You ask me, who am I? I am a wound. You ask me, who am I? I am a flame. You ask me, who am I? I am a tear. You ask me, who am I? I am a bride. You ask me, who am I? I am a sinner God has touched. You ask me, who am I? I'll answer you . . . a fool in love with God.

Stardust and Joy

It seems at times that I am one with the divine Outcast. It seems at times as if I must drink the bitter wine of pain and cry in vain.

It seems at times that I am he in some Gethsemani, staining with bloody sweat the stony hearts of men. It seems at times that I am lifted up, stretched out, nailed on a cross not made of wood but of tepidity. It seems at times that I am entombed in mediocrity. It seems at times that all sorrows and the pain of all the world are mine.

Then suddenly I know it is not so. Then I see but mirrored in me a speck of the infinity of blood, of tears, of pain and death of Christ.

Then I know that even this speck, for me, is being one with his divinity.

A Song Caught by the Wind

I am a song caught by the wind that throws me into space, aloft unto strange heights, so full of grace that I hear myself the song of space and it hears me. Yet in the flesh I walk the earth, an earthling yet a song, caught by the wind or the flame of God.

What can I do; what can I say to those who stay behind and cannot be a song like me, caught by the wind?

I am a dancer on the sea of eternity. I dance and dance upon its waves, a child at play.

What can I do, what can I say to those who stay behind in time and cannot see and cannot dance upon the whole of eternity?

I am a woman in love with God. I live on earth, yet heaven is my abode. I am so free that I can come and go, to and fro, from thence to hence and then begin again.

Men think of me as a stranger, a fool. They do not know I am a song, a dancer, a woman in love with God. The tragedy for me is I cannot tell them to come and be a song, a dance or fall in love with God himself. They are so deaf, they are so dumb, they cannot sing nor hear a song. The face of love they have not seen, for they are blind.

Oh, my Beloved, give them sight, hearing, speech and then may I take them with me into the wind, into eternity and you.

My Room Is a Changeling

My room is a changeling. Now it is just a room. But in seconds it can, it can and it does, change into a hospice, a hostel, an inn to which pain flows like a red, red stream.

My room is a changeling. Now it is just a room. But in seconds it can, it can and it does, change into a cell in which the Lord wants me to pray, to rest, to sleep.

My room is a changeling. Now it is just a room. But in a minute it is the world, the whole of it. I see a billion hands raised up imploring for peace, for food, for rest, for sleep.

My room is a changeling in which I offer God constantly my uselessness, which he uses I do not know how.

I Live on an Island

I live on an island, alone in a house that does not belong to today. It has come from old yesterdays like myself.

My island is wild and untamed, like myself. My house is full of strange dreams, like myself.

Wild things of the forest and air come to rest on my island and know they are safe; it is home. We understand each other, wild things of the forest and air, for I am at home on my island and my island is home to them.

We talk about God, the creator and Father of all. They tell me the secrets of his love for them.

Then we speak of the Virgin whose Child was so fair. They tell me stories she told, which are repeated in forest and high in the air from father to son by wild things that abide there.

I live on an island and learn from trees, flowers and grass the most wonderful secrets of God the Father and Son. And on spring nights they'll whisper in awe, tales of the Holy Spirit whom they know as the blessed Wind.

Often we chant complines together, they and I. As I listen, I know I hear the very echo of God's voice in the night.

The Dying and the Living

He said, "I am the resurrection and the life." I know it now with my whole being, for I have died a thousand deaths and resurrected again.

The dying is for those who spurn love, the living dead. We, who love and are so loved by him, must die for them so that they may be resurrected in him who loved them unto death.

The rhythm of the dying and the living-again is pain, for in such dying and returning to life the soul is torn asunder and cries in anguish. Yet, her cry becomes an alleluia that begs to die again.

Both dying and resurrecting are done in strange and awesome depths that stretch into a desert, cold or hot, that only love can bear. It is not flat but mountainous, with peaks which rise into what are not skies. One dies on peaks; one comes to life again from deeper depths, like tombs.

The journey unto peaks and hence to tombs, is shrouded in the mystery of caritas and cannot be seen nor understood except in faith.

Devouring Heart

The Lord's love is a devouring heat, a furnace that sears and burns. The Lord's love is gentle like a spring breeze that cools and kisses the soul.

The Lord's love is a blinding light that clothes his beloved in golden garments. The Lord's love is darker than darkness, shrouding his trysting place lest his love see his face.

The Lord's love is wood stretching the beloved to his embrace. The Lord's love is the blending of joy and pain that sustains and nourishes the bride till she grows to the height he desires.

The Lord's love is rest and turbulent seas and high winds, for he tests the beloved with storms and rests.

Poverty is the dowry the beloved brings, which the lover gives the beggar maid.

6

My Pains

What Are You Saying?

What are you saying to me, Christ of today, tomorrow, eternity, who is everywhere and in everyone? What are you asking of me, Christ of glory and transcendency, who made yourself solid human flesh so that we could better see, through the mysterious transparency, the Father?

What are you pointing to, my Brother Christ? A steep and narrow path to find that seminarian who said, "You can go to hell." He did not care. What do you want me to do with him and the millions like him?

Oh, it is just him today. I hear. I see. You want me to climb the narrow, steep path of love and heft him upon my back? I have no donkey. I am alone, so it must be just my back.

But no, it is not. The lifting is only into my heart, the inn, and you are the innkeeper of my heart. I hear, my Love, my Brother Christ. You want him in my heart to be healed and cared for.

So all is well and I am off into the narrow, steep path, off into the night of faith.

Caritas Christi

The colors are of early spring: gray, purple, violet. The river reflects them all.

White is the little church, like a paschal candle. It stands on its pedestal of purple brown earth, alive in whiteness and in beauty. Lumen Christi!

His peace indeed is all around, a benediction on the church and brown earth. Pax Christi!

Yet, on this early, lovely, spring eventide, I am as one who is and yet is not. Rabboni!

My soul is filled with tears that crush me to the ground. Lacrimae Christi!

It seems to me that far and near I see sin, pain, unpeace, hunger, thirst. Cold hearts so full of hate make haste to rob and kill truth everywhere. Sanguis Christi!

What shall I do, my Love, to bring your peace to men everywhere? Only one word came to me in answer to my lonely cry — Caritas Christi!

His Pain Is Mine

His pain is mine.

I found Gethsemani in the eyes of a child in a Mexican part of a town. Bloody sweat rolled down my face when I saw a rich woman without grace riding in an expensive car, through poor streets, with a haughty air.

I felt the kiss of whips when my eyes fell on a man who had sold his soul for gold. The crown of thorns ate into my flesh when I looked at hungry youths and saw them fed with stones instead of bread.

The weight of the cross crushed me into the dust when a harlot passed dressed in robes of gold. I was stripped naked when men of God sold him again for pomp and power that weighed more than thirty Roman silver coins.

The nails entered deep into my hands and feet when I beheld parents making their homes hell. I died eight thousand deaths, lifted high up to the sky, when I saw a town cut in two by the bleeding avenue of a color line.

Thus his pain is mine.

Silent and Dark

Silent and dark, the night and I stand listening. For whom? For what? Stormy and passionate, moaning and crying through all the winds, the night and I. For whom? For what?

Lying in the dust of a thousand roads, crouched, spent under our cloak of dark, waiting, the night and I. For whom? For what? Weeping lost tears men call rain, weeping until our hearts break, the night's and mine. For whom? For what? Graceful, expectant, reaching out for stars to bedeck our nakedness. For whom? For what?

Crouching in mortal terror before the dawn, the pale gray dawn of days that will rob the night and me; will rob the night and me of standing still, of listening, of storms, of tears, of stars that clothe her nakedness and mine. Why?

"You foolish heart. Of old and broken things I can make beauty unsurpassed. Behold yourself. Do you not know the answers to your whys and whats and whos?

I cloak you with the night to stand and wait for me. I throw you in the dust of a thousand roads to lift you up to me. I give you tears that men call rain to wash you clean. I send the storms of passion to wake you. The stars, I made to clothe your nakedness and make you fair.

You wait for me, your God, for I can take all those I wish and make them fair beyond all men's dreams and desires.

Yes, foolish heart, I am the Lord your God and I desire with a desire that consumes me to make you mine.

For this, I, the Uncreated, became a man. For this,

I died against an angry sky. For this, I conquered death . . . to make you mine.

I am a jealous God, oh foolish heart, remember that. I want you for myself alone; that is why I use the night, to bring about our union. For I shall use you as I will to do my will. Yours is but to love and to obey.

You shall be my instrument of love, for you and I shall fight for the souls of men, against Satan, the angel of all sin. I yield to him only those who are the truly dead; none others.

So, foolish heart, behold your tremendous Lover and go wherever I shall wish, to fight my battles. With all my goods I you endow. Go forth now. I shall come to you at my good pleasure.

There is no night nor day for you. All are one and all are mine until I shall be yours forever."

Tears

The wind was high. It wept its tears against my door.
It seemed to me these were the tears of all the lost,
the lame, the blind, the sick. The world passed by with
head high and sneering eyes.

I could not sleep. The wind was high and I alone
with all men's tears. What does one do with treasures
such as these?

I lifted each unto the wind and bade it take them to
the Lord to be consoled, healed, made new.

The wind was high. It wept its tears against my door
and then it soared.

Atonement

Somewhere, some time, in the dark of night or the light of a gray day, a silver bird snatched me away. Into dark clouds all lined with black he flew and flew until we left behind the earth and all I knew.

Quite suddenly, the silver bird turned around and began to fall. It fell, as if it were a stone, into some space and depth I had never known.

It seemed I died along the way but then revived. The silver bird seemed to stay forever in this hell without heaven. It was so narrow, hemmed with peaks that had no end. It was so dark that no light sent into these depths a single ray.

I was alone except for fears that sang and sang their endless dirge so full of dry, unshed and heavy tears.

I tried to pray but words and thoughts returned my way and lay around me like pebbles or stones. I was alone. I tried to cry but tears would dry within my soul and rattle there like rattlesnakes, awake, awake. I tried to move, to walk, to talk but I was nailed to mountain tops inverted.

"Is this then hell?" I cried. An echo answered me, "Yes, the hell you have to know, where you have to be, if you want to free priests, wherever they may be."

Tears Again

There is a mystery about tears sometimes, when they appear as a gift divine descending like a torrent or a flood that nothing can deter, stop, dam. They come unbidden, swift. Their flow is free, and yet they are a weight that prostrates a soul to earth and seems to push it into dirt until it is one with it.

There is a mystery about tears sometimes, as if they were not human but divine . . . as if the heart of God could not contain its pain and in his love has found one to share his tears.

There is a mystery about tears sometimes, when one knows without knowing that his soul must cry. For tears like that alone, can pierce a stony heart that does not want to love.

A Thousand Roads

I lay upon the dust of a thousand roads, a bruised and broken thing, of no account. There were no days to brighten my dark and fearsome night. Men passed me by and laughed. Few stopped to see if life had left me; but seeing it had not, shook off the dust of this road or that and went along clicking, clacking their venomous tongues.

I must have risen, walked and stood and walked again, for roads were new, the dust the same. I knew its smell, I knew its taste. It filled the wounds upon my face. It ate itself into my flesh, where rags were thin or torn or rent. Was there an end to roads and dust? Was there an end to this domain of Lady Pain?

I cried and wept in the dark night; but only darkness, dust and pain picked up my endless, weak refrain.

And then one day, that was not day at all but night again, one stopped and stooped to the thing that was myself and said, "Arise and come with me, my love." When I looked up, I saw one who was all beautiful, all light. I was ashamed of wounds and dust, of grimy dirt and of the signs of ugliness darkness had left upon the useless, broken thing that was myself.

Swift was his answer, swift like the wind. He bent to my nothingness and lifted me into infinity. It seemed as if a fire touched my lips and I was lost in ecstasy.

I do not know, I cannot tell the time, the place. One thing I know. I walk in light and garments white and yet the night holds me still tight and Lady Pain shows me more and more of her domain.

But now I know that there is one who will come again, as swift as wind, as clean as rain. And I shall know again, again, the fire and flame of his embrace.

Loneliness

Loneliness like a beast is tearing at my heart, tearing at my heart and succeeding in tearing it apart. How can I live, oh Lord of the pierced heart, when all I have is bleeding morsels for a heart?

Loneliness, like some obscene old woman who prostituted her youth for shillings, pence, rupees, cents, cackles night and day into my ears until my mind weeps silently and hopelessly its bloody tears.

Loneliness comes to me like a ghostly thing, skeleton from a thousand graves, embracing me like lovers do in the dark night. Loneliness sings to me its ghastly lullabies that keep all sleep from me night after night until the sound drives me into surrealistic, frightening dreams without sleep.

How can that be, oh Lord of Gethsemani? There is no olive tree, no stone to receive my bloody sweat, and all around me are people wide awake.

Could it be that their charity is fast asleep and so they cannot see or fathom my agony?

Tormented

I am tormented, tortured by the sight of the poor scavenging for their food in filthy places while others are weight-watching because of gluttony.

I am tormented, tortured by the old, the young, the poor, abiding in our rich cities. I cannot sleep. Their voices, muted by their weakness, their hunger, are dancing in my brain, or is it my heart? Yes, dancing the "danse macabre."

In the lonely night I cry to God for them, my cupped hands offering a ransom not of silver nor of gold but of my tormented self, a reparation for all that has been done to them. Lord have mercy!

7

Prophetic Calls

Asbestos Man

Once in time, unto the earth, Love spilled itself in tongues of fire. Men then became columns of flames that burned without consummation, torches themselves who spilled God's fire wherever they set their sandaled feet.

Today, in our cold, gray, robot age, Love descends in sheets of flames. But modern man wears on his soul an asbestos suit. He walks untouched, unfired, cold, amidst God's fire.

What is to him the Paraclete, when his gloved hand can press a little button and unleash fires that will destroy himself, the earth. All are in his power. He is unto himself, God.

What traffic can godlike man have with the God of myths, nursery rhymes, a hill, a cross, and a foolish spendthrift death? What are to him tongues of fire or sheets of Love's flames? He cannot bother to spell that childish word: Love.

Encased in his asbestos suit he does not know himself. He wears it night and day, his prison; and his safety and his reason are all woven into the very fabric of it all. Around him men cry out in hunger, hunger for love. He does not hear. Nor does he know that his asbestos boots are soaking up their blood, shed in despair. He is immune — or so he thinks — in his asbestos suit.

But soon, so very, very soon, the blood will seep through, for asbestos is so porous it drinks up all moisture. What fire cannot touch, blood will.

Asbestos man, soon you will die, soaked with the blood of brothers you did not know and could not love because you hid yourself in your asbestos suit. Soon you will die, not even knowing where; but it will be upon a hill in Palestine, alone, beneath an empty cross you did not choose to love.

Asbestos man, while you have still some time, little time, tear off your suit and let the sheets of fire renew your soul and make you clean.

Thoughts Upon Seeing the Desert of Arizona

The desert, hot, sandy, scorched by an angry sun, was verdant, cool, compared to the hearts of white men.

Within its vast waste it held in beauty, wild, majestic, the reflection of God's face. The desert of white men's hearts was bleak and dead, reflecting but the light of Lucifer after his fall, which is no light at all. The mesas, mountains, hills, kissed by wind, by rain, knelt on the desert sands like gigantic hermits of old, unceasingly praying to the Lord God.

White men walked God's desert beneath the shadow of the praying hills, like buzzards seeking prey, haughty, proud, with unbending knees, with not a thought of God, the Lord. White men had thrown this desolate land, like bones to dogs, to his own brother, the Indian.

Wounded, silent, strangely meek, blending with sand and tumbleweeds, the Indian lived in this desolate land of thousand shades and endless sand, timeless, praying even as the hills to a God he called "his Brother above."

The Father of all, infinite Lord, watched the praying hills, the sands of gold, the desolate land, lonely and raw, crumbs of his white children picked up by his red.

The hills saw it first, trembled and shook. The sands saw it next and tried to hide in thousand nooks. The anger of the Lord came, a mighty wind leveling cities proud and valleys green, leaving behind the naked white and dead for other deserts to be buried in.

Advent

The world is a Bethlehem where all the inns have no room for him. The canyons of modern cities are caveless, skyscrapers having shuttered their entrances.

The music of the donkey's hoofs is lost in the swoosh of our endless traffic.

Where, then, shall the Woman give birth to the Wonderful One, in this caveless world, in this Bethlehem with inns that have no room for him?

Stop the noise of the traffic! Pause in your goalless rush. Stop, you organization man, drunk with the pride of technological madness that makes you a slave of machines! See your skyscrapers tremble and dissolve in an avalanche of tears before the voice of the Father. He can make the world a cave that will hold your broken mechanical dreams, smashing your silly idols, your spaceships, your robots, your homes, like they were the fragile fruits of potters' wheels.

Stop your noise and listen to the music of a donkey's hoofs bearing the weight of the Woman whose hour has come.

Hasten! Make warm the caves of your souls so that the Holy Anointed One may be born in them — or read the writing of destruction on the eternal walls.

Priests

I saw nothing but bridges, broken down bridges at first but no priests.

Then suddenly, against the dark of the anger of God, I saw my Love, my Lord standing before each bridge, desolate and alone, unable to cross and reach the multitudes waiting hungrily for him on the other side; waiting hungrily, waiting patiently, waiting and weeping and crying for my Lord, my Love to come and feed them and make them his own.

Swiftly I ran to my Lord with a heart full of love and desire, desire to make of myself a bridge for my Lord to cross over. But the voice of my Lord bade me stand still and listen.

He said, "My Father made me a bridge between himself and man's hunger for him. I am the bridge; but it was my wish to make many small bridges across the divide that would carry me, through my sacrament, to satiate the hunger of man whom I love so madly that I made myself helpless, hidden in bread and in wine to be carried to all by my bridges.

But, behold, my little bridges, my beloved bridges are falling down, rotting in pride, in lust and in sloth."

The voice of my Lord died and he fell prostrate to the ground and lay still as one utterly spent but not dead.

In the timeless silence I strained with my whole being filled with love, tears and pain to break the bonds that held me rooted to a spot, to run to my Love; for I knew if I could break those bonds I could find strength to carry my Love to those whom He loved madly — the children of men.

But the voice of my Lord spoke in a whisper, broken

and halting, like the whisper of a dying man. He said, "Be still and understand what my love asks of yours.

Go and repair my bridges, my priests. Repair them by making my sadness your sadness, my passion your passion, my pain your pain, my loneliness yours."

Before the whisper, the broken whisper of my Lord, died in my ears, I cried out, "My Love, give me your sadness, give me your passion, your loneliness and your pain and with them give me your grace to bear them; for I am nothing before your eyes and have my being only in the breath of your grace."

Now my Lord's voice spoke, vibrant and clear and oh so near, "I give you my grace but I will give you more. I will give you myself in a priest who knows me and knows my ways and my desires. I will make him the gardener of your soul which is my enclosed garden, to prune to the quick, to weed and tend and make you fair for myself and teach you the ways of my passion and pain, my loneliness and my sadness; so that one day, if you walk in utter obedience to his will, which is mine, he shall bring you to me as a bride."

All things, sounds and sights vanished for me and I fell like one dead, yet alive, in an ecstasy of love. Again the voice of my Lord bade me to look at the priest who was to lead me to him by the ways of pain, loneliness, sadness, love and passion.

And looking up, I saw no one by my Lord. In the unwalled, unsheltered city of the world, amidst the darkness of its flesh, its pomp, I wandered hungrily, seeking ceaselessly for my Lord's footprints.

Then the voice of my Lord called me to rest in the light, the warmth, the glow of the inexpressible beauty that fills the deep silence that is he. In the utter silence of my Lord, the voice of my Love spoke clearly to me and bade me to look at his priests.

I was loath to lift my eyelids that were heavy with love for him; and for a fraction of an instant I held them tight, tight closed, to hold the intangible beauty of love beneath them. Again the voice of my Lord bade me open my eyes and look at his priests and his voice was filled with a sadness so great that my eyes opened wide and I leaped from the couch of his fragrant silence and looked.

And I saw nothing but bridges, rotting, sagging, un-painted, uncared-for bridges, some covered with the slimy green moss of lust, others leaning drunkenly this way and that, others again painted in the shoddy, cheap colors of pride and desire for power, some just flabby and sloppy with indifference and sloth, lying there as one dead yet alive and all with the same loneliness, the same pain, the same sadness.

Yet even as I looked, I saw a splendor lying like a mantle of golden light about my Lord and in it, I knew it was not he but another like him.

I saw my Lord bend and lift the other up and lay him across the divide, a bridge of surpassing strength and beauty. And I saw my Lord walking, running across this new bridge and I knew it for a priest and my gardener.

I knew that forever it would be thus — he in the priest and the priest in him; both in my Lord's passion and I a garden enclosed and the priest the gardener of it; and forever compassionating, sharing, bearing the burden of both from afar, even as Maria of Magdala did.

My heart is a wanderer now in the unwalled, un-sheltered city of the world, its flesh and pomp. Yet I am not afraid nor weak any more, for my gardener, my priest and my Lord, will prune and weed and lead me across the dark valley and the towering mountains, the dank waters and the slimy marshes, by the light of his spendor which is my Lord's, into the way, first of his loneliness and his pain, then into his arms.

8

To Celebrate or Mourn

Advent

The river freezes. As it does, it sings and sings, for it loves its prison of ice, since the Lord decreed that it should be thus.

The river freezes. As it does, it sings and sings, for it makes a path, white, smooth, for the donkey's hoofs and the Virgin with Child on its back.

The Donkey

Listen. Can you hear the sound of a donkey's hoofs, quite near, quite near? Listen. Blending with them is the sound of a man walking and softly talking.

Let us arise and go and see why this sound fills my heart with ecstasy.

Behold a donkey, a girl and a man walking alone, travelling light in the starry night. Let's go join them and see why so much ecstasy surrounds them.

The Woman is with Child. Where can they go in the dark night that seems so bright? Let us arise and see their journey's end. Come with me. Don't be afraid. They seem to go to Bethlehem. Let us follow them.

The Infant Christ

Somewhere behind the Iron Curtain, forgotten, overlooked amongst the tangles of old woods with faint, crisscrossing paths now unused, the Infant's shrine stands straight and full of grace amidst bowers of fragrant wild flowers.

Few pass it by and those that do look weary, furtive, frightened, half alive. Yet each takes time to pause and look and read words etched by some unknown hand long dead, etched deeply into the very wood that holds the shrine itself aloft.

The words are clear and all can read, "Where people lift their eyes they meet the eyes of God. Look up, you. He is your God. You joyless ones, he understands; they killed his joy too.

"Look up, you too, he is your God; you who are unskilled in the ways of mammon, of buying, selling, trading. They laugh at you, hound you, send you away into dark prisons, for life to stay. He understands; they tried the same with him. He conquered them once. He will conquer them again in you."

Christmas Eve

This is a night of splendor, a night of expectancy and joy all tender. There is in it the scent of a thousand opening flowers and of spring.

How strange, for snow and ice still hold the earth imprisoned. How strange; in the forests trees are still asleep. Nowhere can be seen the smallest green bud.

This is a night of splendor with music in the air. How strange, for beneath the soft light of a moon, all is quiet, white-quilted with snow.

This is a night of splendor, for somewhere it seems a lily regal, slim, is shedding its perfume. How strange, for it is winter. Lilies do not bloom in the snow.

It is a night of splendor, filled with the sound of a donkey's hoofs that walk with a strange, joyful cadence that speaks of glory hidden and other awesome things.

This is a night of splendor, a night of expectancy and joy all tender. Why is it then that my heart wonders if it is ready to be a cradle for a Child?

Easter Vigil in Russia

Twilight is long, the nights are longer, there in Holy Russia. But at long last the darkness falls, bringing silent, recollected, motley crowds into its city streets, its old, mysterious country roads.

The streets are dark. The lamplighter will light them after the Resurrection of the Lord. From the open doorways of churches pour golden streams of light from a thousand candles flooding the outer darkness; and men hasten to be bathed in that holy light.

The singing starts within the golden light. Time ceases to exist as prayer chant grows louder. Hope in the parousia soars like a glowing sword.

Suddenly, all is silence and darkness within the hallowed walls. Slowly the holy mystery of mysteries begins and men light their candles anew at the Christ candle, the Lord.

Melodious, gentle, the choir's voices swell and blend with human souls ascending to God on scales of naked love.

Suddenly the priests sing out, "Christ is risen! Verily he is risen!" Men almost die with joy. All words cease. Alone the "Alleluia" pierces the dawn with its unbearable delight.

Bread, wine, God, I — one. He conquered death. Now he is mine.

The streets are alight with lights. The lamplighters have passed this way.

An Easter Meditation

Rabboni. I see you, gardener of my soul, in splendor clad; and yet my heart is heavy, for I behold your beauty unsurpassed in a thousand hungry faces and I have empty hands.

Rabboni. The alleluias of my joy make jonquil carpets for your pierced feet; and yet my heart weeps before the thousand wounds that cover you in the cold and naked, who stand so silently before my empty hands.

Rabboni. My eyes are dazzled by your resurrected glory — Lumen Christi — and yet my heart beholds the black night of your loneliness in the forsaken who wait for help from my empty hands.

Rabboni. The fragrance of your unguents brings ecstasy to me; yet the bitter-sour smell of your poverty is wafted to me from the endless line of pinched, gray faces of the poor. They cry to me from many places, without words. My answer to them is just a display of empty hands.

Rabboni. Exultant is my soul with songs of gratitude and joy at the conquest of death by you, Lord; yet I see your bloodstained face so still in Mary's hands, in the poor dead. How can I be your Nicodemus and bury them with empty hands?

Rabboni. Will you once more enter through the closed door of human hearts and show them your wounds, your pierced and loving heart and make them see they still must believe your words and you? You have said that all that is done to the least of your brethren is done to you. Then perhaps they will open their hearts and purses and fill my empty hands with silver and gold that will allow us to feed the hungry, clothe the naked, house the forsaken, bury the dead.

Rabboni. Please!

The Passion of God and Man

The First Sad Mystery

The beads fall like thunder. The hands that hold them begin to tremble, each bead an echo of feet upon the earth. How strange that bare feet upon soft ground reverberate like thunder across the arches of time and make hands tremble.

The beads fall like stones splashing into waters deep, a sea quite infinite. But how can a sea be made of the bloody sweat and tears of just one man in agony? And yet it is — the sea of Gethsemani.

The beads are clattering steel that sound like armies on the march; and hands shake and tremble and drop the beads of wood upon a wooden floor. But how can that be? There was no army, just a few soldiers from the high priest's court. Yet the centuries have multiplied them into endless steel-clad cohorts of men that have come to crucify their God.

Such is the first Sad Mystery of the rosary.

The Second Sad Mystery

The knotted cords whistled and fell, not with a smacking sound but with a cutting one. The bones were exposed in patches and here and there the flesh seemed to be hung on them, torn. No cry escaped him, only a moaning, gurgling sound.

It was so long ago, you think. It isn't so. For those who have ears to hear, the sound can be heard at any time. For now the cords are made of souls and the cutting sound is that of their laughter, jeering and unbelief. On a thousand whipping posts Christ is flagellated today and yesterday. There are still tragic places where ragged pieces of flesh and bone adhere to wood. Go over to China and see, or there, behind walls or barbed wire or snow wastes — men hitting God and God not hitting back.

Get out your beads and pray and pray the second most Sorrowful Mystery of the most holy rosary; and put your flesh between the whips of men and God before it is too late.

The Third Sad Mystery

The hands were gloved in steel or iron, that thorns were powerless to pierce. Trained soldier's hands, they twisted the thorns into a crown with a graceful flip. Yet the hands were strong and pitiless, trained to deliver death, or torture foe. They encrowned him with one blow of a mailed fist. Thorns entered the flesh and matted hair and rivulets of blood covered his back, making a cloak of red, long before they put on the purple.

Man crowned God and made him bleed and God stood meek and silent. But from that day, the shadow of a soldier's hand making a crown casts an immense and strange darkness upon the earth and all those who live in it. Thorns that no hand could touch or flip or make into a crown have penetrated the minds of men from then to now and will continue unto the end — unless a few who love will come and with their naked hands pluck out the thorns and make a crown for themselves to atone for the one he wore for love of us.

Behold the long, black, slender thorns of all the fears, guilt and scorn, of all the things unseen that

96

come from the dark depths of men. Behold them gathering and crowning and piercing the minds of men. All those who love, despise, or are tepid to the Son of God and Man, will know, because of this, the sharpness of the thorns unto the end of time.

Yet such is his love — he seeks and seeks souls who will go and pluck with naked hands the living thorns and carry them, a crown upon their heads.

Can't you see why this is the age of fears, seeking, darkness, dread? This is the age of the crowning with thorns, of man who crowned his God. Who loves enough to accept the walking within the third most Sorrowful Mystery of the King?

The Fourth Sad Mystery

Green wood is heavy. The stones are square in spots and sharp. The crowd is close; so is the day. Green wood is heavy on a bloody back. But heavier yet is sin.

Take it apart and look at it, splinter by splinter. Then put it together again and you will not know the secret of the wood, why it can crush the Lord into the depths of hell. If wood could shrink, it would; if wood could weep, it would; if wood could tear itself into nothingness, it would. But it is wood and cannot.

Perhaps it knows why it was so heavy, but it won't tell. The fourth Sad Mystery is locked within its wooden breast and in the flesh of God that bore its weight, the weight of all your sins and mine and all those who came before and will come after. Each man can look and touch the wood and know how much weight he added to it all.

The sins of pride were right inside the spot where the beams met. The sins of lust went in the sharp edge of the transverse beam that cut so deep into the bloody back of God. The sins of sloth filled in the transverse beam from east to west and drunkenness made it uneven so that the weight of it was doubled in some way.

Greed made the upright part and shared it with hypocrisy, uprightness that was so crushing that it made the Lord stumble, fall. All the sins of envy and of judgment were there, where wood and naked feet meet at the heels and they weighed the wood down so as to make the wounds deeper on the sacred feet; they hit so hard while dragging in the dust. The whole of it was like a mantle made of wood that covered him with weight and crushing closeness.

How strange that love is cruciform and so is sin; and that the Lord had to carry it and die on it so as to conquer it and lift it from the souls of men.

The fourth Sad Mystery is written for us in wood.

The Fifth Sad Mystery

The nails were huge, the hammers the Romans used, heavy. The cross, hewn from green wood, lay on the ground.

They laid him on the wood unplaned, full of splinters, big and small. He stretched himself, crossing his feet the way they wanted, laying his hands on the transverse beams, meek as a lamb, which indeed he was.

They hesitated. He seemed so strange, so meek, yet power flowed from him with a force far greater than they could wield with their hammers and other tools.

Slowly, deliberately they drove the nails into the soft flesh of hands, of feet. Can you hear the sound of hammers, the sickening sound of nails entering human flesh?

The crucifixion itself was over. Now to lift him up and place the cross where they had dug a hole for it. It wasn't done gently — oh, not at all! It took six men to lift the burden of the man who also was God.

Finally it was done. Some labourers were made to fill the hole and trample the earth until it was quite hard, firm enough to hold the cross and him.

The fifth Sad Mystery is written for us in nails and flesh.

9

Prayers

Saint Joseph the Unknown

Out of the silence, deep and holy, the gentle Joseph comes; and every movement, every step, even his carriage, speaks of courage, understanding and of love. He is not old, but young and vital; tall, sparse, with hair as soft as silk and dark as night. His eyes are blue, reflecting a glory that is rarely seen, for it has been given to him to father the Son of God without fathering, the only man to whom the Father would entrust his Son.

The bride, the Church, knows him well. It is at Joseph's feet that nightly she lays her burdens, for who better than he, who cradled in his arms the flesh of God, to deal with his mystical body? And her children bring to him thousands of broken dreams, sorrows and hearts that are wounded. Who better than the man who believed the impossible, the craftsman of silence and faith, to answer the prayers of children that walk in darkness alone?

Yet, notwithstanding his glory, his beauty, his light, he is still Joseph the unknown; for silent and humble, he always stands on the side, letting the Mother and Child go ahead of him, for they are his only delight.

But watch! In heaven the Father is touching the iridescent curtain that is so light and so bright that it appears as dark as night. Listen! The touch of the Father has rent the curtain in two and out of its brilliant darkness has come Saint Joseph anew.

This is the hour for the Father to reveal his reflection in the eyes of the man whom he found worthy to father his Son, without fathering. This is the age of Mary and Mary is Joseph's spouse. The Queen of earth and heaven is bound to him by a thousand strands of love that we can't understand. It seems she won't go further unless she has Joseph by her side.

Tall, reflecting the glory of Father, Son and Dove, Saint Joseph, spouse of the Virgin and patron of the bride of Christ — Joseph! Joseph! we need you, we who wander through the darkness of the night unable to find a stable to give birth to the Christ in us. The ends of the world repeat the age-old refrain, "There is no room." How timely is your coming, O Joseph, foster-father of God and of us.

To the Carmel
of North Carolina

A hill and peace. Brick walls, soft red, outline Carmel and close it off from the world's noise and strife. Yet it hurls those who live enclosed inside into the very midst of pain, of tears, and cries of all men's hearts.

Serene they walk, these brown-clad nuns, blending with earth and trees; and yet each nun is just a leaf, storm-tossed by love.

A pain-torn Christ forever dies on their altar crucifix of wood, while each one of them daily drinks the bitter chalice of a pain-filled and living Christ.

I, pilgrim of noisy streets and marketplace, came here to rest upon my Lover's breast and at once I understood that their solitude contained the pain, the noise, the sin, the strife of all the world I knew.

But here all these change into a cross that these brown-clad nuns carry unto the hill of death, of love, of joy. And as they walk, their solitude becomes once more a garden fair where Lover meets beloved.

(To the Carmel of the Most Holy Incarnation, Durham, North Carolina, written during a retreat)

For a Novice
of the Precious Blood

The Lord bent gently to a soul and spanned the infinity that separates Creator and creature with a smile. His voice was ardent, low. "Wilt thou love me alone?" he asked, as lovers do.

The soul, young and shy, feeling the heat and light divine, whispered a "Yes" that only God could hear; it was so low, yet tender, sweet. And now he seemed to come so close that she could touch the Lord of hosts.

He asked again; this time there was a plea in the Lord's voice. "Will you wear red, my love, for me? Will you receive from my own hands a flaming robe of red that will make you one with me in an ecstasy of blood and pain?"

Again the soul so young and shy whispered her "Yes" for God alone to hear and know.

She never knew how swift and passionate was his response. She found herself held in his heart and then she felt the lance, the nails and knew the wood to be her marriage bed.

To the Religious
of the Precious Blood

Oh, solitude, that is not solitude at all, but castle fair, garden enclosed, Love walks with you . . . now all alone, now followed by some saints, or all, by angels and by she who is the Mother of your fair Love, Queen of the universe.

You, whom he called to share garden enclosed and castle fair, do you understand that your land of solitude is not solitude at all but a lovers' tryst, a garden enclosed reserved for those who love well unto the end, a mansion immense with many courts that all lead to the castle's heart, the bridal room?

How long, you ask, must one take, to make the journey from court to room and Groom? The way is short or long, depending on the bride.

Has she left all at the gate, or taken something small with her into that solitude that is not solitude at all?

The Lord of the mansion and of souls is a jealous Lord. He wants her all. Behold, he bids her leave all things behind and come to him naked, meek and mild.

His Mother will clothe her for him at the gate of solitude, that is not solitude at all . . . a bridal robe heavy with the weight of love; his cross, a mantle rare, the color of passion and of blood; a crown of rubies unpolished, brown and dark like thorns that will begin to sparkle when love meets Love.

The way to bridal room and Groom is long or short. Run, Child, and see with your own eyes.

Go to Joseph

Go to Joseph, of course, the young, strong, silent man. His silence, once entered into, heals all it touches. His silence is a school of courage, faith and love. It makes a beautiful bridge between man and God, a bridge we need to find, oh, so terribly much today, when most lives are so empty of God that men have even forgotten the way back to him.

To Joseph, of course, the poor man whose foster Son was born in a stable and whose family lived most frugally in a little forgotten village of Palestine but who held in his arms the wealth of the nations and the light of the world and who can teach us all how to empty our hands of tinsel and fill them with love, faith, and happiness.

To Joseph, of course, the mender of broken toys, furniture, houses, as well as broken hearts, souls, bodies, minds and families. Yes, let us go to Joseph, whom Jesus and Mary love so much.

For a Priest

Maria, beloved, make him all fire, filled with desire to warm the cold hearts of men.

Maria, beloved, give him the gift of tongues to speak of love that dies for love as if he were the lover.

Maria, beloved, pray to your Spouse that he will make him a mighty wind that lifts all men to him who is, who was and ever shall be.

Maria, beloved, give him the gift of pain that sears and cleanses and makes whole again.

Maria, beloved, make him into another Christ, your Son.

JOURNEY INTO CONTEMPLATION $3.95

George A. Maloney, S.J. An in-depth handbook of guidance, inspiration and concrete advice. In it, Father Maloney provides sure teachings on deep union with God, discussing techniques, problems and anticipated rewards. Small groups who pray together contemplatively are also counseled. The author is a master retreat director and writer of many books, including our *The Returning Sun.*

MANNA IN THE DESERT $5.95

George A. Maloney, S.J. The Israelites spent 40 years wandering in the desert, a model of an indeterminate time for all Christians to spend in meeting God in the inner poverty of the desert of our hearts.

This book builds this theme using as a title the words Jesus used to describe Himself as the manna that has come down from heaven to feed hungry Christians in their desert journey to the heavenly Jerusalem. It is a book dealing with contemplative prayer and aims at Christians who have already begun the journey into contemplation. It touches on themes of a desert spirituality such as death-resurrection; weeping and mourning; silence and purification of the senses; prayer as adoration and as entering into the heart of Christ. It challenges growth of the *anima,* the Mary in us, especially as we encounter the crises of limits in our desert journey.

BECOMING A CHRISTIAN PERSON $5.95

Robert E. Lauder. Becoming a Christian person is a lifelong process. The author sees two elements as essential to that process; accepting the Father's love for us and reaching out in loving service to others. Exploring the implications of these two elements, Fr. Lauder discusses the mystery of personal existence, the meaning of death, the significance of the cross in the life of a Christian, the meaning of conscience and the necessity of prayer. All these topics are centered around the theme of Christian personhood.

LOVE IN ACTION $5.95
Reflections on Christian Service

Bernard Hayes, C.R. This book explores the spiritual base out of which all valid ministry must come. Very often, "doing" and "ministering" call for activity which is identical or similar. The difference between doing and ministering lies in the motive behind the activity. One can "do" for many reasons. One can "minister" only out of love. Using the gospel of John, we focus vividly and compellingly on the "why" of Jesus' ministering and we explore the explicit commissioning of the disciples to minister.

FINDING PEACE IN PAIN
$3.50
The Reflections of a Christian Psychotherapist

Yvonne C. Hebert, M.A., M.F.C.C. This book offers a positive approach to overcome the paralyzing effects of emotional hurt in difficult life situations which can't be avoided or changed. Each of the ten chapters clearly illustrates how this form of special prayer can transform life's hurts into opportunities for emotional and spiritual growth. Ms. Hebert draws the reader into the real-life situations of those whom she counsels to join their pain to the sufferings of Christ in His passion.

THIRSTING FOR GOD IN SCRIPTURE
$2.95

James McCaffrey, D.C.D. In this book, the author directs our attention to the Bible as a means of slaking that thirst, as a true source of light for the searching mind and heart. Several texts of Scripture are quoted at length and discussed. The copious references from other texts, not quoted, enable the reader to compare and contrast for him/herself the ways of the Spirit. It is by reading the Bible text itself that the truth and comfort of God's Word may sink into our lives.

PRAYING WITH MARY
$3.50

Msgr. David E. Rosage. This handy little volume offers twenty-four short meditations or contemplations on the key events in the life of our Blessed Mother. The presentation is short, simple and to the point. The object is to turn the user to the New Testament so that he or she can bask in the light of God's Word, grow in love of that Word and respond to it as fully as possible. For a growing insight into Mary's interior life, these short reflections can be very helpful. *Reign of the Sacred Heart.*

RECONCILIATION:
$5.95
The Sacramental Path to Peace

Msgr. David E. Rosage. Many of life's problems stem from strained or fragmented interpersonal relationships caused by anger, pride, jealousy, self-centeredness, etc. We may not readily recognize these causes since we have lost our sense of sin. In this book we gain insight into the merciful heart of Jesus which leads us to appreciate more fully the Sacrament of Penance as a channel of forgiveness and healing and peace.

DESERT HARVEST
$5.95

Rev. Robert Wild. All who desire solitude or those who find themselves in solitude because of life's circumstances will find in this book insights, advice and encouragement. The author shares what he has learned while living in hermitage. Author of *The Post-Charismatic Experience.*

LIVING FLAME PRESS
Box 74, Locust Valley, N.Y. 11560

QUANTITY

_____ Becoming a Christian Person — 5.95
_____ Love in Action — 5.95
_____ Manna in the Desert — 5.95
_____ Reconciliation — 5.95
_____ Post-Charismatic Experience — 4.50
_____ Finding Peace in Pain — 3.50
_____ Thirsting for God in Scripture — 2.95
_____ Praying With Mary — 3.50
_____ Journey Into Contemplation — 3.95
_____ Spiritual Direction — 5.95
_____ Encountering the Lord in Daily Life — 4.50
_____ The Returning Sun — 2.50
_____ Bread for the Eating — 3.50
_____ Living Here and Hereafter — 2.95
_____ Praying With Scripture in the Holy Land — 3.95
_____ Discernment — 3.50
_____ Discovering Pathways to Prayer — 3.95
_____ Mourning: The Healing Journey — 2.95
_____ The Born-Again Catholic — 4.95
_____ Wisdom Instructs Her Children — 3.95
_____ Grains of Wheat — 3.50
_____ Desert Harvest — 5.95

NAME _____

ADDRESS _____

CITY _____ STATE _____ ZIP _____

Kindly include postage and handling on orders. $1.00 on orders up to $10; more
than $10 but less than $50, add 10% of total; over $50, add 8% of total. Cana-
dian residents add 20% exchange rate, plus postage and handling. N.Y. State
residents add 7% tax unless exempt.